10 MINUTE

MINUTE

MOMENTS

SERIES

RENEW

GOD'S MISSION. OUR PURPOSE.

BEING MADE NEW
TEN MINUTES AT A TIME

JAMES GROUT AND BEN STEWART

 simply for students

YouthMinistry.com/TOGETHER

10 Minute Moments: Renew
Being Made New Ten Minutes at a Time

© 2013 James Grout and Ben Stewart

group.com
simplyyouthministry.com

Credits
Authors: James Grout and Ben Stewart
Executive Developer: Nadim Najm
Chief Creative Officer: Joani Schultz
Editor: Rob Cunningham
Cover Art and Production: Veronica Preston

ISBN 978-1-4707-0843-6

10 9 8 7 6 5 4 3 2 1   20 19 18 17 16 15 14 13

Printed in the U.S.A.

CONTENTS

INTRODUCTION

We heard recently that if a YouTube® video runs more than three or four minutes long, people are less likely to click on it because they are unwilling to commit that much time to watching one video. Is that true for you? It often is for us. If either of us is interested in watching a video, we will often look first to see how long it is. If it's too long, we'll pass it up in search of something with the same subject that's a little shorter.

However, we each have also noticed that we're inclined to watch four or five videos in a row, which adds up to about 15 or 20 minutes of our time. So whether we view a 15-minute video or several three-minute videos, the result is the same: We've just watched videos for a quarter of an hour.

If you were told to spend five hours (300 minutes) hearing from and interacting with God, you might find that intimidating and overwhelming. But that's exactly what you can do this month thanks to this book. All you have to do is set aside 10 minutes each day to engage with God through his Word and the devotions in this book—each one written to help you hear from and spend time with God. We encourage you to view those 10-minute moments with God as a daily reminder that he is with you at all times.

"Renew" is not only the title of this book, it is also the overarching theme of the book and shows up on every single page. As you will discover, renewal is a constant theme of the Bible—and even more importantly, renewal is the very heart of God. Our God loves to make things new! As you spend time with God, we hope your eyes will be opened to the ways he brings renewal to this world, to our communities, and to each of his children—including you.

We are trusting God to RENEW you day by day
(2 Corinthians 4:16)!

James and Ben

Day 1

THE BEAUTY OF NEW THINGS

I (James) really like getting something that is new. The first car I ever bought was used—very well used. So were the next four I owned. But a few years ago, I traded in my used car and bought my first new car. It was fresh from the factory: no miles on it, no marks on it, no previous owners, and no funky smells. In fact, it was my first experience with the "new car smell." I was very happy.

You've probably experienced the joy of owning something new as well. Our enjoyment of such things comes from the fact that God created us in his image and he is all about new things. When God created this world and everything was new, he was very pleased with it.

Read through the passage below twice.

Genesis 1:26-31 (NLT)
26 Then God said, "Let us make human beings in our image, to be like us. They will reign over the fish in the sea, the birds in the sky, the livestock, all the wild animals on the earth, and the small animals that scurry along the ground." 27 So God created human beings in his own image. In the image of God he created them; male and female he created them. 28 Then God blessed them and said, "Be fruitful and multiply. Fill the earth and govern it. Reign over the fish in the sea, the birds in the sky, and all the animals

that scurry along the ground." ²⁹Then God said, "Look! I have given you every seed-bearing plant throughout the earth and all the fruit trees for your food. ³⁰And I have given every green plant as food for all the wild animals, the birds in the sky, and the small animals that scurry along the ground—everything that has life." And that is what happened. ³¹Then God looked over all he had made, and he saw that it was very good! And evening passed and morning came, marking the sixth day.

Spend some time reviewing the following questions in relation to the verses you've just read. Write down your answers if it helps you concentrate.

- What does this passage reveal to you about God and his character and his desires?

- What can you discover about humanity from these verses?

- What do these verses tell you about the intended relationship between humanity and God?

- At the end of the sixth day of creation, God saw everything he had made and declared that all of it was good—actually, very good! Is it easy or difficult for you to imagine everything being good? Why?

You and God
- Tell God some of your thoughts about how he created humanity and the role he gave to humans in his creation. Talk to God about something you really loved when it was new—let God know that you can understand a small piece of how he felt when he saw his completed creation.

- If there is some quality about God that you find particularly important in the account of creation, take some time now to tell him what that is and thank him for being that kind of God. Specifically talk with God about why that character quality is so meaningful to you.

- Take about a minute to be silent and listen to what God might want to say to you through his Holy Spirit.

THOUGHTS

This space is here for you to jot down some thoughts, write out a prayer, draw a picture, or do whatever you want to help you remember your 10-minute moment.

Day 2

NO LONGER NEW

Not long after purchasing my brand-new car, I (James) forgot one of the most important rules of the road: Always come to a complete stop at a stop sign. My rolling stop turned into a minor accident as I hit the car in front of me. The damage was not extensive to either car, but I did have to spend a few minutes picking up pieces of my headlights from the gutter. In an instant my new car was no longer new—and it never would be again.

In a similar but much deeper way, that is the effect sin had on God's good creation: It was no longer new and no longer only good! God's perfect creation was tarnished by sin. And humanity's close, intimate relationship with God was interrupted.

2 MINUTES

Read the passage below a couple of times—but don't rush. Absorb the significance of this event.

Genesis 3:1-8 (NLT)
[1]The serpent was the shrewdest of all the wild animals the Lord God had made. One day he asked the woman, "Did God really say you must not eat the fruit from any of the trees in the garden?" [2]"Of course we may eat fruit from the trees in the garden," the woman replied. [3]"It's only the fruit from the tree in the middle of the garden that we are not allowed to eat. God said, 'You must not eat it or even touch it; if you do, you will die.'" [4]"You won't die!" the serpent replied to the woman. [5]"God

knows that your eyes will be opened as soon as you eat it, and you will be like God, knowing both good and evil." ⁶The woman was convinced. She saw that the tree was beautiful and its fruit looked delicious, and she wanted the wisdom it would give her. So she took some of the fruit and ate it. Then she gave some to her husband, who was with her, and he ate it, too. ⁷At that moment their eyes were opened, and they suddenly felt shame at their nakedness. So they sewed fig leaves together to cover themselves. ⁸When the cool evening breezes were blowing, the man and his wife heard the Lord God walking about in the garden. So they hid from the Lord God among the trees.

Spend some time reviewing the following questions in relation to the verses you've just read. Write down your answers if it helps you concentrate.

- Think about the beauty of God's very good creation and all the first man and woman had to enjoy. When and where do you most love to experience God's creation and nature?

- How was the serpent able to convince the woman and man to eat the fruit God had forbidden? Why was his crafty lie so effective?

- When do you find yourself most vulnerable to the enemy's lies and deceptions?

- Why is the shame Adam and Eve felt about being naked an important part of this passage? What had changed?

3 MINUTES

You and God

- Talk to God about some of the sins in your life that make you very aware that you are not "new."

- If you want to ask for forgiveness or for help in the areas where sin seems to have control, God would love to hear that prayer now.

- Be as silent as possible to see if God has anything to say to you through his Spirit.

THOUGHTS

This space is here for you to jot down some thoughts, write out a prayer, draw a picture, or do whatever you want to help you remember your 10-minute moment.

RENEW: MADE NEW AGAIN

Day 3

After banging up my brand-new car, I (James) was sad and embarrassed. More than anything, I just wished the accident had never happened. I wanted my car to be exactly as it was when I first saw it in the showroom. I took the car to be repaired and repainted, and after about a week I got my car back looking really good. A body shop can make a damaged car look like it's new, but that's only a repair job—it's not actually new.

Sin has had a similar effect on our world. We can try to make it look good and pure, but we don't actually have the power or authority to make things new again. That power and authority belong only to the God who created everything in the first place. God made everything and it was very good, but once sin stained and damaged the perfect creation, only God could set things in motion to make everything new again. This happens through Jesus. God came into this world in the form of a man to reverse the effects of the first man's sin. He is in the process of renewing everything.

Read the passage below a few times; these verses come from a paraphrase version of the Bible.

Romans 5:18-21 (The Message)
18-19Here it is in a nutshell: Just as one person did it wrong and got us in all this trouble with sin and death, another person did

it right and got us out of it. But more than just getting us out of trouble, he got us into life! One man said no to God and put many people in the wrong; one man said yes to God and put many in the right. [20-21]*All that passing laws against sin did was produce more lawbreakers. But sin didn't, and doesn't, have a chance in competition with the aggressive forgiveness we call grace. When it's sin versus grace, grace wins hands down. All sin can do is threaten us with death, and that's the end of it. Grace, because God is putting everything together again through the Messiah, invites us into life—a life that goes on and on and on, world without end.*

Spend some time reviewing the following questions in relation to the verses you've just read. Write down your answers if it helps you concentrate.

- These verses draw a comparison between the first man (Adam) and Jesus Christ (sometimes referred to as the Second Adam). In what way are Adam's actions related to the actions of Jesus?

- What is your reaction to the statement that sin doesn't have a chance in comparison with grace (receiving favor we do not deserve)?

- What can sin offer you? What does grace offer?

- Where do you see God doing a work of renewal in this passage? What is God making new?

You and God
- Even though the original sin was not ours personally, you and I have inherited the consequences of sin. This means we have a

sinful nature, and we all sin. If that feels unfair or unreasonable, tell God how you feel about that. If you accept that this is the way it is, then tell God how you feel about your own sin.

- Tell Jesus what you think about his role in making everything new. If you are thankful for his work of renewal in the world and in your life, tell him so.

- Try to be silent for a minute to see if God wants to speak to you through his Holy Spirit.

This space is here for you to jot down some thoughts, write out a prayer, draw a picture, or do whatever you want to help you remember your 10-minute moment.

Day 4

A NEW YOU: SHATTERED EXPECTATIONS

Have you ever been mad at God? Maybe it sounds too harsh to say mad. Have you at least been *disappointed* in God? Perhaps the request you have offered up over and over again has gone unanswered. Or the broken relationship you hoped God would heal remains an open wound. Or you continue to struggle with the same temptation, even though you hoped God would instantaneously take away that desire from your life.

If we're honest, being a Christian doesn't mean things get easier. In fact, sometimes it makes things more frustrating because we feel like God doesn't care or has abandoned us. God just doesn't act the way we expect. But we aren't the first people to experience this: Even Jesus' own disciples had their expectations shattered.

2 MINUTES

Read through the passage below twice.

Matthew 16:21-23 (NLT)
²¹From then on Jesus began to tell his disciples plainly that it was necessary for him to go to Jerusalem, and that he would suffer many terrible things at the hands of the elders, the leading priests, and the teachers of religious law. He would be killed, but on the third day he would be raised from the dead. ²²But Peter took him aside and began to reprimand him for saying such things. "Heaven forbid, Lord," he said. "This will never happen

to you!" 23Jesus turned to Peter and said, "Get away from me, Satan! You are a dangerous trap to me. You are seeing things merely from a human point of view, not from God's."

Spend some time reviewing the following questions in relation to the verses you've just read. Write down your answers if it helps you concentrate.

- Why was Peter so upset by Jesus' statement?

- What expectations do you think Peter had for Jesus? How did Jesus' plan not meet those expectations?

- Have you experienced disappointment? Think of a time when God didn't do what you expected or act the way you had hoped—how did you respond?

- In what area(s) of your life are you more concerned about your will being fulfilled than God's?

- Do you believe God cares about your concerns? What do you think about the idea that God's plans are for your good even when you cannot see the end?

You and God
- Two truths lie side-by-side: God does not disappoint—but we experience disappointment. Talk to God about your understanding of this seeming contradiction.

- Try to spot some areas in your heart and mind where you have expectations of God that are really just self-serving. Ask God to change your expectations and make his good plans clear to you. Thank him for being the God who *"causes everything to work together for the good of those who love God and are called according to his purpose for them" (Romans 8:28 NLT).*

- Take one final minute to be silent and see what God may want to speak to you by his Spirit.

This space is here for you to jot down some thoughts, write out a prayer, draw a picture, or do whatever you want to help you remember your 10-minute moment.

Day 5

A NEW YOU: REAL COMMITMENT

When a person becomes a follower of Jesus, that decision brings along more than just a title or label. Claiming the name *Christian* means you are deciding to follow Jesus—to live a new kind of life. The word *Christian* actually means "little Christ." It was originally a term of ridicule or shame from the Romans, but the early church eventually owned that title and turned it into a name of honor.

Little Christ: one who is committed to living the way of Jesus.

Picture a young boy trying to be like his big brother. He copies his moves, listens to the same music, and uses the same words. He thinks so highly of his big brother that he wants to be just like him.

2 MINUTES

Read through the passage below several times.

John 6:60-69 (NLT)

60Many of his disciples said, "This is very hard to understand. How can anyone accept it?" 61Jesus was aware that his disciples were complaining, so he said to them, "Does this offend you? 62Then what will you think if you see the Son of Man ascend to heaven again? 63The Spirit alone gives eternal life. Human effort accomplishes nothing. And the very words I have spoken to you are spirit and life. 64But some of you do not believe me." (For Jesus knew from the beginning which ones didn't believe, and

13

he knew who would betray him.) *65Then he said, "That is why I said that people can't come to me unless the Father gives them to me." 66At this point many of his disciples turned away and deserted him. 67Then Jesus turned to the Twelve and asked, "Are you also going to leave?" 68Simon Peter replied, "Lord, to whom would we go? You have the words that give eternal life. 69We believe, and we know you are the Holy One of God."*

5 MINUTES

It's important for us to acknowledge that all-out commitment to Jesus is not easy. Certainly, we experience beautiful moments in being a Christ-follower, but when we understand the life we have been called to live and what it looks like to imitate Jesus, it's not always easy. In this passage, we see that many of Jesus' disciples discovered this truth and decided to throw in the towel and leave.

Spend some time reviewing the following questions in relation to the verses you've just read. Write down your answers if it helps you concentrate.

- What parts of following Jesus do you enjoy? When do you find it most difficult? You may want to write these things down.

- As you look at your journey with Jesus, have you ever found yourself in a place where you wanted to give up? Are you in that place right now?

- How do you think we can get through those difficult times? How can Scripture, prayer, and talking with other Christ-followers help you in those times?

3 MINUTES

You and God

- Tell Jesus about the hardest moments you face when following him. Ask him to open your eyes to the ways he wants to be with you in those moments.

- Ask for strength from God to continue following Christ even when it is difficult.

- If you are able to agree with Jesus' closest disciples, say these words to Jesus: "Where else can I go? You have the words of eternal life."

- Take a moment to be quiet and receive strength or comfort from the Holy Spirit.

TH●UGHTS

This space is here for you to jot down some thoughts, write out a prayer, draw a picture, or do whatever you want to help you remember your 10-minute moment.

Day 6

A NEW YOU: WHO ARE YOU... REALLY?

Identity is really important. Think about how you relate to your friends. So much seems to depend on how people view you. The people you hang out with, what you wear, and the activities you get involved in—they all can seemingly define you. Teenage years can be brutal when it comes to identity. With one word someone can destroy your identity. One wrong choice can create an unwanted identity. A misunderstanding can label you something you're not. Of course, you can always fake your identity.

1 MINUTES

Read through the passage below several times. It's also a good portion of Scripture to memorize.

Genesis 1:26-27 (NLT)

26Then God said, "Let us make human beings in our image, to be like us. They will reign over the fish in the sea, the birds in the sky, the livestock, all the wild animals on the earth, and the small animals that scurry along the ground." 27So God created human beings in his own image. In the image of God he created them; male and female he created them.

6 MINUTES

Spend some time thinking about the things below and answering the questions in relation to the verses you've just read. Write down your answers if it helps you concentrate.

This passage is incredibly essential to our understanding of identity. At the beginning of history, during creation, God made this incredible statement, and the implication of this statement is that you get your identity from him!

This means two things: First, in God alone you will find who you are, what your purpose is, how you were intended to live, and what it means to experience total satisfaction with your life. Second, if you expect to find those things anywhere else, you *will* be disappointed!

- What do you honestly think your friends, peers, and those around you see as your identity? What words would they use to describe you?

- Are these the words you want them to use? If not, what would you prefer they say about you?

- What might it look like to allow God to define your identity? What words might God use to describe you?

3 MINUTES

You and God
- If you want to know what God has to say about who you are, take time to read these verses: Romans 8:1, 39; 2 Corinthians 5:17; Galatians 3:26; Ephesians 1:7; 2:13; and 2 Timothy 1:1.

- If you're tired of trying to establish your identity through what you do or the people you hang out with, ask God to show you what it looks like to be identified through him.

17

- Take a moment to be quiet and listen to what God might want to tell you about what he sees when he looks at you.

This space is here for you to jot down some thoughts, write out a prayer, draw a picture, or do whatever you want to help you remember your 10-minute moment.

A NEW YOU: FAITH AND DOUBT

Recently my (Ben here) 8-year-old son expressed some doubt about the existence of God. If Santa Claus and the Easter Bunny are not real, then (logically, in his mind) how can God be real? You can't see God either! As a parent my initial reaction was to totally freak out—on the inside, of course!

Doubt can lead to some scary places. It can cause us to question the existence of God or his love for us. Doubt might cause us to question whether or not God truly intends all things for good to those that love him. But I have learned through my own experiences that doubt actually can be a healthy part of real faith.

2 MINUTES

Read through the passage below twice.

Mark 9:17-24 (NLT)
[17]One of the men in the crowd spoke up and said, "Teacher, I brought my son so you could heal him. He is possessed by an evil spirit that won't let him talk. [18]And whenever this spirit seizes him, it throws him violently to the ground. Then he foams at the mouth and grinds his teeth and becomes rigid. So I asked your disciples to cast out the evil spirit, but they couldn't do it." [19]Jesus said to them, "You faithless people! How long must I be with you? How long must I put up with you? Bring the boy to me." [20]So they brought the boy. But when the evil spirit saw Jesus, it

threw the child into a violent convulsion, and he fell to the ground, writhing and foaming at the mouth. [21]"How long has this been happening?" Jesus asked the boy's father. He replied, "Since he was a little boy. [22]The spirit often throws him into the fire or into water, trying to kill him. Have mercy on us and help us, if you can." [23]"What do you mean, 'If I can'?" Jesus asked. "Anything is possible if a person believes." [24]The father instantly cried out, "I do believe, but help me overcome my unbelief!"

Spend some time reviewing the following questions in relation to the verses you've just read. Write down your answers if it helps you concentrate.

- When you read these verses, what do you imagine the man was expecting when he came to Jesus? Do you think he was 100 percent confident he would get what he came for?

- How was his unbelief connected to his belief? How is it possible that the two can co-exist?

- Do you ever doubt God? If so, in what ways? If not, how have you heard your friends express their doubts?

- Does doubt keep you from trusting and pursuing God? Do you believe God can help you overcome your unbelief?

You and God
- Ask God to help you think about someone who might be a safe person with whom you could share your doubts.

- Hebrews 11:1 defines faith as "confidence in what we hope for and assurance about what we do not see." Tell God about your hopes and ask him to give you confidence and assurance.

- See if you can form a prayer about renewing your faith in God.

- Listen quietly for a minute to see what God might want to tell you to strengthen your faith.

This space is here for you to jot down some thoughts, write out a prayer, draw a picture, or do whatever you want to help you remember your 10-minute moment.

A LIFE MADE NEW: ZACCHAEUS (PART 1)

This true story of one man's encounter with Jesus is one of the most encouraging events recorded in the Bible. Zacchaeus, the man who encountered Jesus, was not the greatest guy. In fact, many people who personally knew him probably thought of him as the worst person they'd ever met. He was a Jewish man but worked for the hated Romans collecting taxes from his fellow Jews. Most of the money went to Caesar, but tax collectors always kept extra for themselves. As the chief tax collector, Zacchaeus got paid by all of the other tax collectors. He was rich, but he was also a traitor and a thief!

So why use the word *encouraging* when describing this man's experience? You'll have to see how the event ends to fully understand, but it's amazing to see the way Jesus treated the "chief" traitor and thief. It means there is hope for anyone and everyone—regardless of how we have lived life up to this point!

Read through the passage below twice. Try to imagine the scene; draw a picture if it helps you visualize what you have read.

Luke 19:1-4 (NLT)
¹Jesus entered Jericho and made his way through the town. ²There was a man there named Zacchaeus. He was the chief tax collector in the region, and he had become very rich. ³He tried to get a look at Jesus, but he was too short to see over the crowd.

4So he ran ahead and climbed a sycamore-fig tree beside the road, for Jesus was going to pass that way.

Spend some time reviewing the following questions in relation to the verses you've just read. Write down your answers if it helps you concentrate.

- The crowds were big in Jericho that day—and elsewhere in the Gospels, we read about multitudes of people flocking to Jesus. What made Jesus so appealing? Why were people drawn to him?

- What do you think Jesus was thinking as he looked at the crowd that day? Based on what you know from the Gospels, what emotions might Jesus have experienced as he saw people with spiritual needs?

- Zacchaeus was just another face in the crowd—in fact, he was a face hidden by the crowd. What draws people to desperately seek Jesus? When have you passionately pursued him?

- When do you find yourself most naturally and easily worshipping Jesus?

You and God
- If it has been a while since you felt excitement at getting to "see" Jesus, talk to him about what has dulled your enthusiasm.

- Many of the people crowding Jesus that day wanted to see the man who was also God. They probably wanted to worship him—because God is worthy of our worship. Spend some time worshipping Jesus right now by thanking him for how he is

23

working in your life and by telling him all of the reasons you look forward to seeing him face to face.

- Take a moment and listen to what the Holy Spirit may want to say to you.

This space is here for you to jot down some thoughts, write out a prayer, draw a picture, or do whatever you want to help you remember your 10-minute moment.

A LIFE MADE NEW: ZACCHAEUS (PART 2)

Do you know the feeling of being chosen for something meaningful or memorable? When picking teams on the playground, you were chosen first (or at least you weren't chosen last). When interviewing for a job with several other applicants, your name was called. There was only one dessert left, and your parents gave it to you instead of your brother. Being chosen feels good.

Today, as you continue reading through the account of Zacchaeus, imagine how he felt being chosen by Jesus. Other people in the crowd probably would have gladly hosted Jesus in their homes, too, but Jesus picked Zacchaeus. Jesus willingly associated himself with a "notorious sinner."

If you are a follower of Jesus, you are chosen, too. But being chosen by Christ is so much better than being selected for the sports team or getting the last dessert; it's the very pathway to a new life. And ultimately, the call to follow Jesus goes out to everyone—it isn't limited to a select few.

2 MINUTES

Read through the passage twice (the first four verses are a repeat from yesterday, but read through them again as a reminder of how the passage starts).

Luke 19:1-7 (NLT)

¹Jesus entered Jericho and made his way through the town. ²There was a man there named Zacchaeus. He was the chief tax collector in the region, and he had become very rich. ³He tried to get a look at Jesus, but he was too short to see over the crowd. ⁴So he ran ahead and climbed a sycamore-fig tree beside the road, for Jesus was going to pass that way. ⁵When Jesus came by, he looked up at Zacchaeus and called him by name. "Zacchaeus!" he said. "Quick, come down! I must be a guest in your home today." ⁶Zacchaeus quickly climbed down and took Jesus to his house in great excitement and joy. ⁷But the people were displeased. "He has gone to be the guest of a notorious sinner," they grumbled.

Spend some time reviewing the following questions in relation to the verses you've just read. Write down your answers if it helps you concentrate.

- It appears that Jesus had never met Zacchaeus before, yet he called him by name when he passed under the tree. When has Jesus done something unexpected in your life?

- Jesus said he *must* be a guest in Zacchaeus' house that day. Why do you think he was so insistent?

- Being acknowledged and chosen by Jesus was amazing for Zacchaeus. What kind of treatment do society's "outcasts" and "sinners" typically receive from people—including religious people?

- How much of a risk was Jesus taking with his own reputation by choosing Zacchaeus, a "notorious sinner"? Why was Jesus willing to take that risk then—and still willing to take that risk today?

You and God

- Zacchaeus was not really worthy of being chosen by Jesus for a dinner party that night—but neither were the people in the crowd who thought they were better than Zacchaeus. In fact, no one is worthy (because of our sin), yet Jesus chooses to offer us forgiveness and wants to spend time with us anyway. Tell God how you feel about that truth.

- Talk to Jesus about your impression of his decision to spend time with Zacchaeus. Tell Jesus how it makes you feel knowing how he treats people with love, dignity, compassion, and respect—and ask for his help in treating people that way, too.

- Listen for a moment to see if God is trying to tell you anything through his Holy Spirit.

This space is here for you to jot down some thoughts, write out a prayer, draw a picture, or do whatever you want to help you remember your 10-minute moment.

The feeling of being lost is scary. We aren't talking about that time you got confused in the mall parking garage and couldn't remember if you were on the orange or blue level. We're talking about the kind of lost where you aren't sure if you will survive. That scary kind of lost happens when you're hiking in the mountains at night and a storm approaches, and you realize you don't know the way back to your starting point. You begin to suspect that you are going the wrong direction and then it seems you are walking in circles (you probably are).

When someone is that lost, fear can set in—and survival becomes essential. However, sometimes people are that lost but don't even know it. They think everything is fine and they are just happy going along whatever path they find themselves on—even though that path is dangerous, risky, and perilous.

Spiritually speaking, Zacchaeus was that kind of lost. He was a wealthy man with some authority and power. That sounds like a successful person—not someone who is lost! As you read the whole passage today, look for signs of one who was lost (even though he didn't know it) and what it means to be found and saved.

2 MINUTES

Read the whole account of Zacchaeus twice (the first seven verses are a repeat from yesterday).

Luke 19:1-10 (NLT)

¹Jesus entered Jericho and made his way through the town. ²There was a man there named Zacchaeus. He was the chief tax collector in the region, and he had become very rich. ³He tried to get a look at Jesus, but he was too short to see over the crowd. ⁴So he ran ahead and climbed a sycamore-fig tree beside the road, for Jesus was going to pass that way. ⁵When Jesus came by, he looked up at Zacchaeus and called him by name. "Zacchaeus!" he said. "Quick, come down! I must be a guest in your home today." ⁶Zacchaeus quickly climbed down and took Jesus to his house in great excitement and joy. ⁷But the people were displeased. "He has gone to be the guest of a notorious sinner," they grumbled. ⁸Meanwhile, Zacchaeus stood before the Lord and said, "I will give half my wealth to the poor, Lord, and if I have cheated people on their taxes, I will give them back four times as much!" ⁹Jesus responded, "Salvation has come to this home today, for this man has shown himself to be a true son of Abraham. ¹⁰For the Son of Man came to seek and save those who are lost."

5 MINUTES

Spend some time reviewing the following questions in relation to the verses you've just read. Write down your answers if it helps you concentrate.

- Why do so many people believe they will find true joy and contentment through their position, wealth, family, and possessions—but then discover that they can't?

- When Zacchaeus started to make promises about giving money away and repaying those he had cheated, he suddenly became over-the-top generous. How and why can an encounter with Jesus change your attitude toward material possessions?

- The title "true son of Abraham" is so important to this man who was commonly known as a traitor because Abraham was the ancestral "father" of the Jewish people. What name or title could

Jesus speak over you that would be especially meaningful and powerful?

- Jesus' statement about seeking and saving the lost was a reference to Zacchaeus, but it had a broader message, too— what do you think it means for the rest of the world?

- What similarities do you see between what Jesus did for Zacchaeus and what he has done (or wants to do) for you?

You and God

- Talk to Jesus about what it means to you that his mission in this world was to find and save people who are spiritually lost.

- If you feel lost right, now tell God about that and ask that he would remind you that you are not alone.

- Spend some time listening to what the Spirit of God may want to say to you.

This space is here for you to jot down some thoughts, write out a prayer, draw a picture, or do whatever you want to help you remember your 10-minute moment.

A NEW COMMUNITY: RIGHT WHERE I BELONG

Day 11

In Los Angeles there's a place known as the Magic Castle, and although it sounds like something for children, the Magic Castle is primarily for grown-ups to watch magicians and illusionists perform. You don't have to be a magician to belong—but it does help if you can make *something* disappear!

In the world of magic, belonging to this particular group is important. There are requirements to get in, fees to be paid, standards to be kept, and rules to be observed. But although there are costs, there are also benefits. And if you want to even attempt to be anyone in the world of magic, you need to belong to this club!

Read through the passages below a few times (memorize them if you can).

Psalm 100:3 (NLT)
Acknowledge that the Lord is God! He made us, and we are his. We are his people, the sheep of his pasture.

Ephesians 1:6-7 (NLT)
⁶So we praise God for the glorious grace he has poured out on us who belong to his dear Son. ⁷He is so rich in kindness and grace that he purchased our freedom with the blood of his Son and forgave our sins.

31

Did you catch that? We are *his*! We belong to God.

Similar to a membership at the Magic Castle, there is a cost to belong to God, but it's not one that *you* have to pay. Jesus has paid the price. There isn't a list of criteria you must check off. No level of perfection attained, skills perfected, or behavior modified. You belong to God—not an elite club, a social group, or even a movement. Simply God. When we truly belong to God, the benefits are amazing! Purpose. Forgiveness. Freedom. Love. Protection. Provision. Mercy. No condemnation. New identity. Eternity with God. The list goes on.

Take a moment to think through the following questions. Write down your answers if it helps you concentrate.

- It's a simple but essential question: Do you belong to God? If so, on what basis?

- Do you ever feel like you are trying to perform for God's approval? What do you think today's passages say about that?

- What part does Jesus play in connecting us to God the Father?

- The benefits of belonging to God are wonderful and humbling! Which two or three benefits mean the most to you? Why?

You and God
- You were made by God, and because of Jesus you belong to God. Take some time to thank God that you belong to him, no matter what! Tell God how you feel about belonging to him.

32

- Think through your life, and ask God to reveal ways you rely more on your performance, rather than on faith in the work of Jesus. Ask God to help you in any areas he identifies.

- Take about a minute to be silent and listen to what God might want to say to you through his Holy Spirit.

This space is here for you to jot down some thoughts, write out a prayer, draw a picture, or do whatever you want to help you remember your 10-minute moment.

Day 12

A NEW COMMUNITY: FORGIVING EACH OTHER

When I (Ben) was in junior high, a friend said some things that really hurt my feelings and did significant damage to my self-image. I was angry and hurt. The pain was intensified because he was my friend and a fellow Christian. For a long time I did not want to forgive him. Even now, as an adult, I sometimes catch myself replaying that scene and feeling some of the same pain I felt when the wound was fresh. Today's passage (and others like it) helped me recognize my bitterness and begin to take steps to forgive and to be healed.

Read through the passage below several times.

Ephesians 4:31-32 (NLT)
31Get rid of all bitterness, rage, anger, harsh words, and slander, as well as all types of evil behavior. 32Instead, be kind to each other, tenderhearted, forgiving one another, just as God through Christ has forgiven you.

Spend some time reviewing the following questions in relation to the verses you've just read. Write down your answers if it helps you concentrate.

- How do the actions and attitudes in verse 31 draw you away from God? How do the actions and attitudes in verse 32 draw you toward him?

- Have you drawn a line to determine who is worthy of your compassion and forgiveness, and who isn't? If so, where is the line?

- Why is God's forgiveness the motivation for our own kind actions toward others? Does this make it easier for you to forgive and be compassionate? Why or why not?

- What might be the ultimate result if you decide to never forgive someone who has hurt you?

- Think of someone that has hurt you in some way. What would it look like to show that person compassion and kindness instead of anger and bitterness? What is keeping you from doing this?

- Do you feel forgiven by God? Why or why not?

You and God

- Ask God to change your heart toward people you find it hard to forgive. Ask God to replace your bitterness and anger with compassion and kindness. Ask God to give you the ability to forgive.

- Write out what you would say if you were able to forgive someone who has harmed you. Pray that God would give you the desire and courage to say those things.

- Take about a minute to be silent and listen to what God might want to say to you through his Holy Spirit about forgiving others.

THOUGHTS

This space is here for you to jot down some thoughts, write out a prayer, draw a picture, or do whatever you want to help you remember your 10-minute moment.

Day 13

A NEW COMMUNITY: WE ARE FAMILY

My wife (Ben here) grew up with two sisters and a brother. They had good relationships with each other and their parents. Their home was a stable environment all through their childhood and teen years. But 15 years ago, her brother suddenly left. He walked away from the family, and none of them have heard from him since then. Not surprisingly, this one decision had a major impact on the rest of the family.

But here's the reality: Even though he walked away, my brother-in-law's status has not changed. He is still the son of his parents. He is still a brother to his sisters. He's not living like it, but he is still a member of that family. How do I know this? Because his parents and sisters still love and miss him deeply.

Read through the passage below twice.

Galatians 4:4-7 (NLT)

⁴But when the right time came, God sent his Son, born of a woman, subject to the law. ⁵God sent him to buy freedom for us who were slaves to the law, so that he could adopt us as his very own children. ⁶And because we are his children, God has sent the Spirit of his Son into our hearts, prompting us to call out, "Abba, Father." ⁷Now you are no longer a slave but God's own child. And since you are his child, God has made you his heir.

Being adopted by God changes everything about your life—your past, present, and future are all significantly altered. Additionally, your family changes. Suddenly you have a multitude of brothers and sisters who share the same Heavenly Father. The choices you make have an impact on their lives, for better or worse.

Spend some time reviewing the following questions in relation to the verses you've just read. Write down your answers if it helps you concentrate.

- According to today's verses, how are we connected to God and each other once we become followers of Christ?

- What things do you appreciate about your biological family? What things frustrate you?

- The church is the family of God. How connected are you to God's family?

- In what ways do you show encouragement and love to the brothers and sisters around you?

- If you've walked away from God's family, what are the reasons? What keeps you from going back?

3 MINUTES

You and God

My brother-in-law (whom I have yet to meet!) has left his family. But he probably doesn't even realize what he's missing out on: wedding celebrations, the birth of a new niece or nephew, graduations, family get-togethers, a group of people who would support him no matter what—the list goes on and on. The same is true with our spiritual family. The moment you commit yourself to Jesus, you have full access to the joys of being part of God's family. When you try to separate yourself from this family, you miss out on awesome benefits—and others miss out on you!

- Take a few moments to tell God what it means to you that he has adopted you as his son or daughter and that you belong to him, no matter what.

- Name some of the people in your life who have cared for you—those who are biological family members and those who are spiritual family members through Christ. Thank God for them and their role in your life.

- Write down one way you can demonstrate what it means to be a supportive family member to someone in your church this week.

- Take about a minute to be silent and listen to what God might want to say to you through the Holy Spirit.

THOUGHTS

This space is here for you to jot down some thoughts, write out a prayer, draw a picture, or do whatever you want to help you remember your 10-minute moment.

A NEW COMMUNITY WELCOME HOME

Day 14

What do you love most about being at home? Or do you love it? For some of you, home might be a great place where you feel relaxed, safe, and able to enjoy a lot of comforts—homemade meals, anyone? But for others of you, home might be an awful place: screaming, verbal teardowns, fear—or worse.

Today's verses come right after the author—the Apostle Paul—explains how Jesus reunites us with God through Jesus' sacrifice on the cross. In other words, when people become followers of Christ, not only are they given a new family, but they also belong to a new household.

2 MINUTES

Read through the passage below a few times.

Ephesians 2:19-20 (NLT)

¹⁹So now you Gentiles are no longer strangers and foreigners. You are citizens along with all of God's holy people. You are members of God's family. ²⁰Together, we are his house, built on the foundation of the apostles and the prophets. And the cornerstone is Christ Jesus himself.

5 MINUTES

Spend some time reviewing the following questions in relation to the verses you've just read. Write down your answers if it helps you concentrate.

- The house of God is meant to be a place of peace, love, and encouragement. When have you experienced this? When has your experience been something quite different?

- In what specific ways are you contributing to God's family? Are your contributions positive? negative? nothing?

- What are some specific ways you can help your local church—God's family—be a place where there truly are no strangers or foreigners?

- If your earthly home is a source of anguish and fear, are you able to find comfort in the household of God—other Christians, church community, a small group?

- How are you building your life on the cornerstone of Jesus?

3 MINUTES

You and God
- Spend a few minutes either thanking God for your earthly home or asking him to renew it—or both.

- Ask God to show you some ways to bring renewal to your earthly home and your spiritual home.

- Take about a minute to be silent and listen to what God might want to say to you through his Holy Spirit.

THOUGHTS

This space is here for you to jot down some thoughts, write out a prayer, draw a picture, or do whatever you want to help you remember your 10-minute moment.

A LIFE MADE NEW: PETER (PART 1)

Meeting someone who is famous can be really exciting. If you have ever met a famous person or even seen one walking down the street, you probably remember that moment well. It's possible you've told the story of that encounter over and over—perhaps embellishing the details each time. This is sometimes known as a "brush with greatness"—and the level of "greatness" depends largely on the identity of the famous person.

A man named Peter probably had the best "brush with greatness" anyone could ever have. Only a few people on earth knew Jesus well, and Peter was one of them. Stop and think about that for a moment: The very Creator of the universe became a man, lived a life without flaw, performed mind-blowing miracles, and finally demonstrated his absolute authority over *everything* by rising from the dead—and Peter got to hang out with him for three years. It sounds like an amazing life, doesn't it? However, Peter's relationship with Jesus had some ups and downs. As we look at how Peter's "brush with greatness" affected his life, see if you notice some similarities to your own encounter with Jesus.

2 MINUTES

Read through the passage below twice.

Matthew 16:13-18 (NLT)
¹³When Jesus came to the region of Caesarea Philippi, he asked his disciples, "Who do people say that the Son of Man is?"

14"Well," they replied, "some say John the Baptist, some say Elijah, and others say Jeremiah or one of the other prophets." 15Then he asked them, "But who do you say I am?" 16Simon Peter answered, "You are the Messiah, the Son of the living God." 17Jesus replied, "You are blessed, Simon son of John, because my Father in heaven has revealed this to you. You did not learn this from any human being. 18Now I say to you that you are Peter (which means 'rock'), and upon this rock I will build my church, and all the powers of hell will not conquer it."

Spend some time reviewing the following questions in relation to the verses you've just read. Write down your answers if it helps you concentrate.

- If you were sitting face to face with Jesus, how would you answer his question in verse 15?

- Jesus knew who he was, so why would he quiz his friends about his identity and who people thought he might be? What did Jesus understand about good questions that we sometimes forget?

- The disciples' answers revealed that there were many different opinions about who Jesus actually was—what kinds of answers would that question get if you asked people at your school who Jesus really is?

- It appears that Simon, who was known as Peter from this point on, gave the only correct answer to the questions posed by Jesus. What was different about his answer? Why did the identity of Jesus even matter?

- Why is it significant that Jesus commended Peter and spoke a blessing over him?

- Why did Jesus say Peter was blessed? Do you think it's always necessary for God to reveal truth to you, or can you figure it out on your own?

You and God
Jesus spoke a word of prophecy over Peter, indicating that he would somehow be foundational in the building of the church— the worldwide community of those who follow Jesus, not a physical building.

- Talk to Jesus about your experience with the church. Tell him about the good and the bad—he can handle the truth.

- If you are confused about why God would entrust his plans to us as flawed humans, tell him about that confusion.

- If you feel privileged to be included in God's work through the church, thank him for choosing you.

- Listen for a moment to see if the Holy Spirit has anything to say to you.

THOUGHTS

This space is here for you to jot down some thoughts, write out a prayer, draw a picture, or do whatever you want to help you remember your 10-minute moment.

A LIFE MADE NEW: PETER (PART 2)

Day 16

Sometimes we choose to do things we know are not right or good:

- We say things we know are untrue.

- We cheat—just a little—to get a better grade.

- We take or keep something that does not belong to us.

- We hurt others in order to feel better about ourselves.

If you can relate to one (or all) of the things listed above, then you probably can also relate to the feeling of shame that often accompanies these choices. The shame comes from knowing what is right but stubbornly choosing what is wrong.

Yesterday you read about one of the most amazing experiences Peter had with Jesus. Today you'll read about the worst moment Peter had in a face-to-face conversation with Jesus. This moment would lead to the greatest shame Peter ever felt.

2 MINUTES

Read through the passage below twice.

Matthew 26:31-35 (NLT)
[31]On the way, Jesus told them, "Tonight all of you will desert me. For the Scriptures say, 'God will strike the Shepherd, and

the sheep of the flock will be scattered.' ³²*But after I have been raised from the dead, I will go ahead of you to Galilee and meet you there."* ³³*Peter declared, "Even if everyone else deserts you, I will never desert you."* ³⁴*Jesus replied, "I tell you the truth, Peter—this very night, before the rooster crows, you will deny three times that you even know me."* ³⁵*"No!" Peter insisted. "Even if I have to die with you, I will never deny you!" And all the other disciples vowed the same.*

Spend some time reviewing the following questions in relation to the verses you've just read. Write down your answers if it helps you concentrate.

- What was the bad news/good news of Jesus' words to his followers? Which part do you think they might have heard most clearly? Why?

- Is it wrong or risky to make promises to God that are fueled by our emotions? Why or why not?

- In contrast to the blessing Jesus spoke over Peter in yesterday's passage, why were Jesus' words to Peter so surprising and shocking?

- Peter's denial of knowing Jesus—which is recorded in Matthew 26:69-75—reminds us that even when we have the best intentions, we still may make the wrong choice. In what way can you relate to Peter's sinful choice and subsequent shame?

- Where in your life do sinful and shameful choices seem to win out over your best intentions? Make a list if it helps you to be more honest.

3 MINUTES

You and God

- Spend a minute or two being honest with God about the sinful choices you have made even when you knew they were wrong. If you are sorry for those choices, ask for his forgiveness.

- If you have accepted the gift of forgiveness and salvation through Jesus' death on the cross—a substitute for our own death, what we deserve for our sin—understand that you are forgiven for the things you have done. God is not going to punish you; he poured out that punishment on Jesus in the crucifixion. You can just receive God's forgiveness now, knowing that he does not hold a grudge.

- Listen for a moment to hear what your forgiving God may want to tell you by his Spirit.

THOUGHTS

This space is here for you to jot down some thoughts, write out a prayer, draw a picture, or do whatever you want to help you remember your 10-minute moment.

At some point in your life, you have probably experienced the amazing feeling that comes from getting a second chance. The whole class failed the test, but the teacher has everyone take it again. Your team missed a critical free throw, but someone on the opposing team stepped into the lane too soon, so you can take the shot again. You hurt a close friend, but after you apologized, the relationship is restored.

Peter had done the worst he could do. He had denied knowing Jesus three times—even though he truly loved Jesus and intended to stick by him. The hurt, disappointment, and shame were overwhelming. Scripture doesn't tell us this, but we're pretty sure Peter was just wishing he could have another chance to make things right.

Read through the passage below twice.

John 21:15-19 (NLT)

15After breakfast Jesus asked Simon Peter, "Simon son of John, do you love me more than these?" "Yes, Lord," Peter replied, "you know I love you." "Then feed my lambs," Jesus told him. 16Jesus repeated the question: "Simon son of John, do you love me?" "Yes, Lord," Peter said, "you know I love you." "Then take care of my sheep," Jesus said. 17A third time he asked him, "Simon son of John, do you love me?" Peter was hurt that Jesus asked the question a third time. He said, "Lord, you know everything. You know that I love you." Jesus said, "Then feed my sheep. [18]*"I tell you the truth, when you were young, you were able to do as you liked; you dressed yourself and went wherever you wanted to go. But when you are old, you will stretch out your hands, and others will dress you and take you where you don't want to go."* [19]*Jesus said this to let him know by what kind of death he would glorify God. Then Jesus told him, "Follow me."*

Spend some time reviewing the following questions in relation to the verses you've just read. Write down your answers if it helps you concentrate.

- When has someone given you a second chance, and what did you learn from that experience?

- After denying even knowing Jesus, Peter found himself sitting with Jesus eating breakfast. What is the greatest life lesson or spiritual truth you have learned through an awkward conversation or encounter?

- Does it seem strange to you that Jesus asked Peter the same question over and over? Why or why not?

- Who are Jesus' sheep—and what are some specific ways *you* can feed them?

- Jesus said Peter would die a similar death to the one he had just experienced. Does it take more faith to live life knowing what the future holds or being unaware what will happen to you down the road? Why?

3 MINUTES

You and God

- Each of us is undeserving of God's forgiveness, but he has extended it to us through Jesus. Talk to God about your understanding of this "ultimate" second chance.

- If there is anything about Peter's story that makes you love Jesus even more, tell him about it. This is called worship—so worship Jesus for a while.

- Take a moment to be silent and hear what the Spirit of God may want to tell you.

THOUGHTS

This space is here for you to jot down some thoughts, write out a prayer, draw a picture, or do whatever you want to help you remember your 10-minute moment.

Day 18

A NEW WORLD: VERY GOOD NEWS

Our world is in desperate need of some good news. Network news programs and cable news channels are filled with reports of wars, shootings, natural disasters, terrorist attacks, human trafficking, water crisis, and more. So the world searches elsewhere to find good news: money, possessions, charity, success, sex, substances, and whatever else we think may reveal "good news."

You may know today's passage well—or the first verse, at least—but don't skim past its life-altering significance. Pay particular attention to the last part of the second verse: *God didn't send Jesus to judge and condemn us, but to save us!*

Read through the passage below several times.

John 3:16-17 (NLT)
[16]"For God loved the world so much that he gave his one and only Son, so that everyone who believes in him will not perish but have eternal life. [17]God sent his Son into the world not to judge the world, but to save the world through him."

Spend some time reviewing the following questions in relation to the verses you've just read. Write down your answers if it helps you concentrate.

- Why do you think verse 16 is so well-known—but verse 17 isn't?

- As you were reading and rereading this passage, what significant word or truth stood out? Why was it so significant?

- The world needs to hear the gospel—the good news described in these verses—but do you need to hear it, too? Do you believe in the good news of Jesus and that there is nothing better this world could offer?

- If the gospel is the best news ever, what are ways God might use you to get it out there? Identify one or two specific things you could do to give others a chance to hear this good news.

- A person can both proclaim the gospel through words and live the gospel through deeds. Which do you find is more natural for you? Do you do it?

3 MINUTES

You and God
- Use this time right now to thank God for the good news! Really dwell on the fact that God sent his Son to save you, not condemn you! Relish in this good news and praise God for it!

- Think through how this good news impacts (or could impact) the way you live. Write out some practical ways it changes (or could change) your life.

- Take about a minute to be silent and listen to what God might want to say to you through his Holy Spirit.

This space is here for you to jot down some thoughts, write out a prayer, draw a picture, or do whatever you want to help you remember your 10-minute moment.

A NEW WORLD: ON A MISSION FROM GOD

Day 19

In 1980, the phrase "We're on a mission from God" was coined in the comedy movie *The Blues Brothers*. The "mission" for the Blues Brothers was to get all the guys from their old blues band back together. Whether or not that mission was actually from God is probably up for debate, but every Christian also finds himself or herself on a mission from God—or perhaps it's more appropriate to say we are on a mission *with* God.

The moment you commit your life to God through Christ, you join God's mission to renew all things. In fact, the question is not "Are you on a mission?" The question is, "How much does the mission you're on impact the way you live?"

2 MINUTES

Read through the passage below a few times, and underline words or phrase that seem particularly important.

Acts 1:6-8 (NLT)

⁶So when the apostles were with Jesus, they kept asking him, "Lord, has the time come for you to free Israel and restore our kingdom?" ⁷He replied, "The Father alone has the authority to set those dates and times, and they are not for you to know. ⁸But you will receive power when the Holy Spirit comes upon you. And you will be my witnesses, telling people about me everywhere—in Jerusalem, throughout Judea, in Samaria, and to the ends of the earth."

5 MINUTES

Spend some time reviewing the following questions in relation to the verses you've just read. Write down your answers if it helps you concentrate.

- Did you know you were on a mission with God? If not, how does this realization change things for you?

- Being a witness includes knowing the truth, believing the truth, and living the truth. Which of those do you struggle with the most?

- You have been called to be a witness in your world. That can mean going to people far away, but it can also mean reaching out to people who are incredibly close to you. Where and to whom is God calling you to be a witness?

- Does knowing that the mission to renew all things is straight from the heart of God change the way you look at your part in that mission? Why or why not?

3 MINUTES

You and God
The fact that God has chosen you to be part of his mission should be humbling! God didn't have to do it that way, but he chose to. It can give you a sense of purpose and clarity on how to live your life.

- Take some time to thank God for choosing to include you in his mission. Thank God for this purpose and singular goal for your life.

- Think through ways that God might be calling you to live out his mission. Is it through a lifestyle change? Is God calling you to

58

give something up? Does he want you to pray differently? Has God placed someone in your life so you can be a "witness" of who Jesus really is? Write out some thoughts about that.

- Take about a minute to be silent and listen to what God might want to say to you through the Holy Spirit.

This space is here for you to jot down some thoughts, write out a prayer, draw a picture, or do whatever you want to help you remember your 10-minute moment.

Day 20

A NEW WORLD: LIGHT

In God's mission to renew the world, there are three major parts. First, God used the nation of Israel as a "light" to the nations around them. Through holy and pure living, they were to show the world what God was really like. When Israel failed to be that light, it set the stage for the second part: God sent Jesus as the light of the world, the one who would come into the darkness (John 1:1-9). But it doesn't end there.

Read through the passage below two or three times.

Matthew 5:14-16 (NLT)
14 "You are the light of the world—like a city on a hilltop that cannot be hidden. 15 No one lights a lamp and then puts it under a basket. Instead, a lamp is placed on a stand, where it gives light to everyone in the house. 16 In the same way, let your good deeds shine out for all to see, so that everyone will praise your heavenly Father."

This truth is amazing. Jesus is saying that God chose us to be his light in this world. That means he reveals the truth of his grace and forgiveness, through us, to those around us. This is a very weighty responsibility yet also an incredible opportunity to let

God's light shine! There can be something about the way we live that unmistakably reveals God's nature.

Take a moment to think through the following questions. Write down your answers if it helps you concentrate.

- God has called you to be his light in a dark world. What might it look like to be that light? What things can you choose to do that will be light to this world?

- What are some things that might "hide" your light?

- Which is more common for you: to reveal the light of God, or to hide the light of God? Is there anything you would like to change about that?

- If you know someone who constantly reveals the light of God in the way they live and talk, what are some of the characteristics of that person that you would like to imitate?

3 MINUTES

You and God

You are meant to shine the light of Christ through your life. The analogy has been made of the light from the moon. When you see the light from the moon, it's not the moon's light, but a reflection of the sun's light. Likewise, you don't produce your own light. The light that is meant to attract others is a light not of your own. What draws people to you is when they see Christ in your life.

- Talk to God about the opportunity he has given to you to be part of his mission. Confess to God what a humbling and weighty task this is and how much you need his help to carry it out!

- If there are times when you would rather hide your light, tell God about that. Ask God for strength and courage to stay on his mission during those moments.

- Take about a minute to be silent and listen to what God might want to say to you through the Holy Spirit.

THOUGHTS

This space is here for you to jot down some thoughts, write out a prayer, draw a picture, or do whatever you want to help you remember your 10-minute moment.

Day 21

A NEW WORLD: HOW DOES IT END?

You're probably guilty—as we are—of trying this little trick at least once: skipping to the end of a book you haven't read in order to write a paper. It is helpful, at least in theory, to know the ending if you are going to try to convince someone that you know the whole story. This may or may not have worked for you when it came to getting a decent grade on your paper, but it does point to this important truth: Knowing how the story ends really matters!

2 MINUTES

Read through the passage below twice.

Revelation 21:1-5 (NLT)

¹Then I saw a new heaven and a new earth, for the old heaven and the old earth had disappeared. And the sea was also gone. ²And I saw the holy city, the New Jerusalem, coming down from God out of heaven like a bride beautifully dressed for her husband. ³I heard a loud shout from the throne, saying, "Look, God's home is now among his people! He will live with them, and they will be his people. God himself will be with them. ⁴He will wipe every tear from their eyes, and there will be no more death or sorrow or crying or pain. All these things are gone forever." ⁵And the one sitting on the throne said, "Look, I am making everything new!" And then he said to me, "Write this down, for what I tell you is trustworthy and true."

5 MINUTES

Spend some time reviewing the following questions in relation to the verses you've just read. Write down your answers if it helps you concentrate.

- Does it give you comfort to know that in the end God is going to make everything new? Why or why not?

- What do you think of the description of life once God has made his home among the people?

- How does knowing the way the story ends change your perspective on life—or does it?

- Where do you need God's trustworthy and true words to be revealed in your life?

- God is going to make all things new. God is going to dwell with his people. God is going to wipe away every tear and there will be no more pain. Of these truths, which brings you the most hope, and why?

3 MINUTES

You and God
- Thank God that one day he will make all things new while wiping away every tear and removing our pain. Ask God for a "taste" of that day even now.

- Talk to God about people in your life who do not know him and may not be prepared for the end. Ask God for opportunities to help them meet and know the one who loves them and wants to make everything new for them as well.

- Take about a minute to be silent and listen to what God might want to say to you through the Holy Spirit.

This space is here for you to jot down some thoughts, write out a prayer, draw a picture, or do whatever you want to help you remember your 10-minute moment.

Day 22

A NEW LIFE: THE LAME MAN (PART 1)

In the beginning of time God made everything new. When our sin brought death and destruction into the world, God began his work of making everything new again! Over the next three days we are going to see the effect God's work of renewal had on one individual. This is the account of a man who could not walk. In fact, he had never walked—not once since birth. While we might see that as a tragic story, God had a different perspective. God saw the man born lame as one more opportunity to do his good work of making everything new again.

2 MINUTES

Read through the passage below a few times, and then underline or circle your favorite part.

Acts 3:1-2 (NLT)

¹Peter and John went to the Temple one afternoon to take part in the three o'clock prayer service. ²As they approached the Temple, a man lame from birth was being carried in. Each day he was put beside the Temple gate, the one called the Beautiful Gate, so he could beg from the people going into the Temple.

66

5 MINUTES

Spend some time reviewing the following questions in relation to the verses you've just read. Write down your answers if it helps you concentrate.

- What do you imagine the life of the lame man looked like from day to day? Write down everything that you think would have been a part of his daily schedule.

- How does the sight of someone who cannot walk affect you? How does the sight of someone begging for money or food affect you?

- When God looks at a person who is in great need, how do you think he views them? Why?

- In what ways have you found yourself treating begging or needy people differently? In what specific and meaningful ways might you be able to help people in these situations?

3 MINUTES

You and God

- To see someone in need is a test of our capacity to love. If you have trouble feeling or acting in a loving way toward the neediest people around you, talk to God about that. Ask him for help in viewing everyone as useful and worthy of love.

- If needs in your life are physically, mentally, or emotionally crippling you, tell God about those areas. God knows and wants to hear you express your feelings.

- Listen for a moment to see if God has anything to say to you through his Spirit.

THOUGHTS

This space is here for you to jot down some thoughts, write out a prayer, draw a picture, or do whatever you want to help you remember your 10-minute moment.

Day 23

A NEW LIFE: THE LAME MAN (PART 2)

When I (James) was a child, I really wanted a racetrack with remote-control cars. I had seen them on TV and knew exactly which one I wanted. However, I was pretty sure I wasn't going to get one because they were so expensive. I lowered my expectations significantly, hoping to get a smaller and less expensive version of the racetrack I wanted. When our neighbors—whose sons were older—gave us their old set, it was so much more than I had expected. I was hoping for a small track with a couple of cars, but I got a huge and winding track with four lanes of remote-control racecars.

The crippled man in Acts 3 had something he wanted (and needed) from everyone who passed by on his or her way into the temple. He had expectations, but they were pretty low. He really just wanted enough money to survive one more day. His expectations could never have lived up to what he received when he met Peter and John—and when he heard the name of Jesus Christ.

2 MINUTES

Read through the passage below (verses 1-2 are repeated from yesterday).

Acts 3:1-8 (NLT)
¹Peter and John went to the Temple one afternoon to take part in the three o'clock prayer service. ²As they approached the Temple, a man lame from birth was being carried in. Each day

he was put beside the Temple gate, the one called the Beautiful Gate, so he could beg from the people going into the Temple. ³When he saw Peter and John about to enter, he asked them for some money. ⁴Peter and John looked at him intently, and Peter said, "Look at us!" ⁵The lame man looked at them eagerly, expecting some money. ⁶But Peter said, "I don't have any silver or gold for you. But I'll give you what I have. In the name of Jesus Christ the Nazarene, get up and walk!" ⁷Then Peter took the lame man by the right hand and helped him up. And as he did, the man's feet and ankles were instantly healed and strengthened. ⁸He jumped up, stood on his feet, and began to walk! Then, walking, leaping, and praising God, he went into the Temple with them.

Spend some time reviewing the following questions in relation to the verses you've just read. Write down your answers if it helps you concentrate.

- When have you looked beyond an obvious need in someone's life and identified a deeper, truer need—or when has that happened to you? What did you learn from that experience?

- Do you think the man was disappointed when Peter and John said they didn't have money for him? Why or why not?

- When has God blessed you in a way that far exceeded what you had expected or requested?

- How do you know the difference between a want and a need in your life? Do you think God cares about your wants as much as he cares about your needs? Why or why not?

3 MINUTES

You and God

- If you are in need today, call out to God. Tell him about your need and ask him to meet it. Remember that "needs" and "wants" are not always the same thing.

- If you believe that there is power in the name of Jesus to meet you where your greatest needs are, tell Jesus you believe. If you are unsure about the power and authority Jesus has in this world, tell him about that.

- Take a moment to ask Jesus to reveal his power in your life and circumstances through the Holy Spirit.

THOUGHTS

This space is here for you to jot down some thoughts, write out a prayer, draw a picture, or do whatever you want to help you remember your 10-minute moment.

Day 24

A NEW LIFE: THE LAME MAN (PART 3)

What amazes you? We each have met people who are easily amazed. The newest gadget on a TV shopping network, an illusionist's slight of hand, a really good burrito—any of these things can be "amazing" for some. Other people are a little more skeptical and possibly even cynical. It seems nothing amazes them, no matter how spectacular it is.

Whether easily amazed or mostly skeptical, we all have moments when the supernatural catches us off guard and amazes us. A mere glimpse of God and the renewing work he does in this world is enough to take our breath away. If you are the skeptical type and wonder if God will ever amaze you, think about the people in this Scripture who witnessed the power of the name of Jesus. At least a few of them were probably skeptics by nature—but all of them were amazed.

Read through the verses below, underlining things you like in this Scripture (you are rereading the first part of the passage).

Acts 3:1-10 (NLT)

¹Peter and John went to the Temple one afternoon to take part in the three o'clock prayer service. ²As they approached the Temple, a man lame from birth was being carried in. Each day he was put beside the Temple gate, the one called the Beautiful Gate, so he could beg from the people going into the Temple. ³When he saw Peter and John about to enter, he asked them for some money. *4Peter and John looked at him intently, and Peter said, "Look at us!" 5The lame man looked at them eagerly, expecting some money. 6But Peter said, "I don't have any silver or gold for you. But I'll give you what I have. In the name of Jesus Christ the Nazarene, get up and walk!" 7Then Peter took the lame man by the right hand and helped him up. And as he did, the man's feet and ankles were instantly healed and strengthened. 8He jumped up, stood on his feet, and began to walk! Then, walking, leaping, and praising God, he went into the Temple with them. 9All the people saw him walking and heard him praising God. 10When they realized he was the lame beggar they had seen so often at the Beautiful Gate, they were absolutely astounded!*

5 MINUTES

Spend some time reviewing the following questions in relation to the verses you've just read. Write down your answers if it helps you concentrate.

- People turned to look when the man first started to walk, run, leap, and praise God. What's the most amazing thing you've seen God do? How did you respond?

- Why were the people so surprised to see where the noise was coming from? What had been their only experience with this man up to this point?

- How do our past experiences sometimes limit our expectations for what God can do?

- Why are many people surprised when they see God do something amazing?

- What amazing thing are you hoping, praying, and believing for God to do in your life or in someone else's life? What would be a great way to celebrate when you experience this answered prayer from God?

3 MINUTES

You and God

- If you have not done it recently (or ever), take some time to worship God for his amazing work of making things new. If you have specific examples of that work from your own life, thank God purposely for those.

- If you are wondering if you will ever witness God's astounding work, tell him about that. Let God know how you wish to know and see his power in the world and in your life.

- Listen for a moment to see what the Holy Spirit might want to reveal to you.

This space is here for you to jot down some thoughts, write out a prayer, draw a picture, or do whatever you want to help you remember your 10-minute moment.

A NEW LIFE: THE LAME MAN (PART 4)

Steven Spielberg, Bill Gates, Oprah Winfrey, LeBron James—these names carry some power and authority. If you owned a restaurant and saw any one of these names on your reservation list, you'd likely set up your best table and tell your chef to create something magical for the menu. By their name alone, celebrities are able to receive special treatment almost everywhere they go. If they are willing to put their name on a product—shoes, cars, shampoo, gadgets—customers are much more likely to buy the product. A name can be powerful.

In the account of the man born lame, Peter and John used the name of Jesus when telling him to get up and walk. The people who witnessed the miracle were amazed. However, there were some religious leaders who believed they were the only authority, and they wanted to ask Peter and John where their authority came from.

Read through the passage below. You may want to reread Acts 3:1-10 first (that was yesterday's reading).

Acts 4:5-10 (NLT)

⁵The next day the council of all the rulers and elders and teachers of religious law met in Jerusalem. ⁶Annas the high priest was there, along with Caiaphas, John, Alexander, and other relatives of the high priest. ⁷They brought in the two disciples and demanded, "By what power, or in whose name, have you done this?" [8]Then Peter, filled with the Holy Spirit, said to them, "Rulers and elders of our people, [9]are we being questioned today because we've done a good deed for a crippled man? Do you want to know how he was healed? [10]Let me clearly state to all of you and to all the people of Israel that he was healed by the powerful name of Jesus Christ the Nazarene, the man you crucified but whom God raised from the dead."

4 MINUTES

Spend some time reviewing the following questions in relation to the verses you've just read. Write down your answers if it helps you concentrate.

- What do you think made the religious leaders so upset? Why were they not thrilled and amazed—as others were—when they heard about the miracle of a lame man who could now walk?

- The passage clearly reveals that the powerful religious leaders did not intimidate Peter. What situations or people can intimidate you when you're preparing to share the good news of Jesus? How can God help you in those moments?

- Why is the name of Jesus so powerful? What is true about him that is not true of anyone else?

- Do you believe the name of Jesus still holds the same power and authority? Why or why not?

3 MINUTES

You and God
- Talk to God about the difficult things in your life that seem too big for you to fix or change. Ask him, in the name of Jesus, to do his renewing work in those areas.

- Thank God for always being with you through the presence of his Spirit. Talk to the Holy Spirit (he hears your prayers) and ask for the confidence he gives in the face of intimidating circumstances.

This space is here for you to jot down some thoughts, write out a prayer, draw a picture, or do whatever you want to help you remember your 10-minute moment.

A GOOD FOLLOWER

Who are you? Someone once asked me that question and I (James) gave several answers that had to do with my job, my house, my education, and my family. But I was told that none of these truly answered the question. All I had told him was what I did, where I lived, what I knew, and to whom I was related. I had not told him *who I was*.

Who you are is called your "identity," and your identity is not something you can easily undo. When we believe and have faith in the good news that Jesus came into the world to reverse the curse of sin, we have a new identity found only in him. Part of that identity is that we are now followers of Christ, his disciples.

Read and then reread the passage below for a couple of minutes. Underline or circle anything that stands out as particularly important.

Matthew 28:18-20 (NLT)

18Jesus came and told his disciples, "I have been given all authority in heaven and on earth. 19Therefore, go and make disciples of all the nations, baptizing them in the name of the Father and the Son and the Holy Spirit. 20Teach these new disciples to obey all the commands I have given you. And be sure of this: I am with you always, even to the end of the age."

5 MINUTES

Spend some time reviewing the following questions in relation to the verses you've just read. Write down your answers if it helps you concentrate.

- These verses are sometimes called the Great Commission. What does that mean to you? What is a commission, and what makes this one "great"?

- If you were a follower of Jesus hearing him tell you this for the first time, would you have been inspired or afraid? Why? What might you have done next?

- The people Jesus was speaking to were his followers, his disciples. Why did he tell them to make more disciples? If we are disciples—our identity as followers of Jesus—then how does this commission relate to us?

3 MINUTES

You and God
- If you consider yourself a follower of Jesus, ask him to show you what it means for you to make disciples—to help others identify with and follow Jesus.

- Ask God to constantly remind you of your identity as one who learns from Jesus and obeys his commission and commands.

- Spend a moment in silence to hear from God as he may want to reveal some truth to you through the Holy Spirit.

THOUGHTS

This space is here for you to jot down some thoughts, write out a prayer, draw a picture, or do whatever you want to help you remember your 10-minute moment.

Day 27

THE REAL CHURCH

Identity theft. We hear warnings about this all the time on TV and in the news. "Make sure you protect your identity," we are told. "If you don't, someone could steal your identity and use it to drain your bank account and run up outrageous credit card bills in your name." I (James) never used to give this any thought at all. I had no fear of identity theft—chances are you don't either.

But then one day I received a call from my bank asking if I had just purchased a $700 airline ticket at the Sydney airport in Australia! I had not—someone pretending to be me was using my credit card number. Suddenly I cared a lot about identity theft!

False identities can be used in very damaging ways. This is true of our identity as Christ-followers, too. When Jesus is our Lord, we are now identified as his body—also known as the church. But sometimes we think church is just about a religious service or a place where weddings and funerals take place. That would be a false identity. A much better and more accurate image of the church is that of a family—not a building, meeting space, or an organization, but a family.

2. MINUTES

Read through the following passages about our status as God's family; make note of anything related to our status as children or brothers and sisters.

1 John 3:1-3 (NLT)

¹See how very much our Father loves us, for he calls us his children, and that is what we are! But the people who belong to this world don't recognize that we are God's children because they don't know him. ²Dear friends, we are already God's children, but he has not yet shown us what we will be like when Christ appears. But we do know that we will be like him, for we will see him as he really is. ³And all who have this eager expectation will keep themselves pure, just as he is pure.

Romans 8:14-17 (NLT)

¹⁴For all who are led by the Spirit of God are children of God. ¹⁵So you have not received a spirit that makes you fearful slaves. Instead, you received God's Spirit when he adopted you as his own children. Now we call him, "Abba, Father." ¹⁶For his Spirit joins with our spirit to affirm that we are God's children. ¹⁷And since we are his children, we are his heirs. In fact, together with Christ we are heirs of God's glory. But if we are to share his glory, we must also share his suffering.

Galatians 3:26-27 (NLT)

²⁶For you are all children of God through faith in Christ Jesus. ²⁷And all who have been united with Christ in baptism have put on Christ, like putting on new clothes.

1 John 3:17-18 (NLT)

¹⁷If someone has enough money to live well and sees a brother or sister in need but shows no compassion—how can God's love be in that person? ¹⁸Dear children, let's not merely say that we love each other; let us show the truth by our actions.

Spend some time reviewing the following questions in relation to the verses you've just read. Write down your answers if it helps you concentrate.

- Adopted children are legally exactly like biological children, and a healthy family always loves them equally. With that in mind, what does it mean to you to be adopted by God?

- What did God think of his Son, Jesus? (See Luke 3:22 if you need help.) How do you think God views you, his adopted child?

- What would healthy family relationships look like among God's children? How should members of the church—the family of God—treat one another?

3 MINUTES

You and God

- Take a moment to talk to God as your perfect Father. Tell God what it means to you that he chose to adopt you into his family.

- If there is another member of God's family you have been mistreating or ignoring, ask for forgiveness—and for an opportunity to make that relationship right.

- Take a minute of silence to hear from your Father.

THOUGHTS

This space is here for you to jot down some thoughts, write out a prayer, draw a picture, or do whatever you want to help you remember your 10-minute moment.

Day 28

SERVICE WITH ABSOLUTE ABANDON

One of the easiest events to plan for any school, church, youth group, or community organization is a service project. They are hugely popular, and people—especially teenagers—love participating in them. This has not always been true. Just a few years ago, it seemed like a bribe was required before students would do service projects. "If you help out this Friday we promise you'll get pizza and we can go to a movie later."

What changed? People could offer many answers to that question, but the ultimate outcome is that today's teenagers are interested in making a difference in the world around them. But does doing a service project make you a servant? Is that the extent of what servanthood is all about? "Servant" is another piece of the identity we have because of our relationship with God through Jesus. As we see what kind of a servant Jesus was, we gain a clearer understanding of what it means to be a servant as he was a servant.

Read through the passage below several times—but don't rush. Underline key words.

Philippians 2:5-8 (NLT)
⁵You must have the same attitude that Christ Jesus had. ⁶Though he was God, he did not think of equality with God as something to cling to. ⁷Instead, he gave up his divine privileges; he took the humble position of a slave and was born as a human being.

When he appeared in human form, [8]he humbled himself in obedience to God and died a criminal's death on a cross.

Spend some time reviewing the following questions in relation to the verses you've just read. Write down your answers if it helps you concentrate.

- This passage helps us focus on our relationships with other Christ-followers—our brothers and sisters in God's family. What is the key to appropriate relationships in this family?

- In your own words, what mindset did Jesus have in relation to others? Do you think it is easy for Christ's disciples to adopt this same mindset? Why or why not?

- For Jesus, how was becoming human the same as becoming a servant? Why was it such a humbling act?

- What does Jesus' death on a cross have to do with being a servant? We are not commanded to die on a cross, but what implications are there for us in that act of obedience?

You and God
- Talk to Jesus about how his decision to offer his whole life as an act of service has affected you.

- As you think about what your life would look like if offered as an act of service, ask God to show you how that might appear.

- Take some time to be quiet and listen to what God might want to say to you through his Spirit.

THOUGHTS

This space is here for you to jot down some thoughts, write out a prayer, draw a picture, or do whatever you want to help you remember your 10-minute moment.

Day 29

THE UNEXPECTED IDENTITY

Do you like the *Mission Impossible* movies? They are based on an old TV show, but there really isn't any comparison. The movies are filled with so much adrenaline-producing action that they make the old show feel painfully slow. However, one line that always showed up in the weekly show was the recorded message telling agent Ethan Hunt of his next mission. The message—which would self-destruct after being played—always included the phrase: "Your mission, should you choose to accept it...." Apparently, Agent Hunt had the option of declining the mission (because presumably it would be impossible), but he never exercised that option. He always accepted the mission.

God has a mission in this world, and God has given this mission to all those who have become his adopted children through faith in Jesus. Here's the twist: Christ-followers don't have the option of declining. God's mission isn't one he gives us if we choose to accept; God's mission is the mission we have already accepted! The mission is now a part of our identity.

2 MINUTES

Read through the passage below two or three times. Underline anything that seems like it might have to do with God's mission in this world.

2 Corinthians 5:17-20 (NLT)
¹⁷This means that anyone who belongs to Christ has become a new person. The old life is gone; a new life has begun! ¹⁸And all

of this is a gift from God, who brought us back to himself through Christ. And God has given us this task of reconciling people to him. ¹⁹For God was in Christ, reconciling the world to himself, no longer counting people's sins against them. And he gave us this wonderful message of reconciliation. ²⁰So we are Christ's ambassadors; God is making his appeal through us. We speak for Christ when we plead, "Come back to God!"

5 MINUTES

Spend some time reviewing the following questions in relation to the verses you've just read. Write down your answers if it helps you concentrate.

- What do you think it means that belonging to Christ brings new creation? What is gone, and what has now arrived in this act of renewal?

- Reconciliation is the act of making peace where conflict has existed. God is all about being reconciled with his creation. Our sin created conflict between God and us, but God has done something to fix that. How did he this?

- Scripture reveals that God's plan for reconciliation is to include us. How does that happen? What is the appeal God is making through us?

- To be an ambassador for Christ is the same as being a missionary for Christ. How does this challenge you to think differently about what it means to be a missionary?

3 MINUTES

You and God

- Talk to God about what it means for you to have peace with him even though you are a sinner.

- Tell God about some friends or family members you know who have not yet been reconciled to him. Ask for a vision of how you could be an ambassador for God in the lives of those individuals.

- Listen for a while to what God might want to speak into your heart.

THOUGHTS

This space is here for you to jot down some thoughts, write out a prayer, draw a picture, or do whatever you want to help you remember your 10-minute moment.

Day 30 — NEW IN EVERY WAY

This is it. This is the final day of your 30-day exploration of God's heart for all things new. We hope that through these daily moments, you have experienced a new relationship with God.

Think of these past 30 days as the beginning of a new way to live. Instead of living life trying to "do your best" or "behave," live in communion with God. That means thinking first about being with God rather than trying to act a certain way. We are convinced that if each of us lives with the constant reminder that God is alive within us by his Spirit, we won't need to worry about our behavior—it will reflect the very presence of God in us.

Read through the verses below several times; it would be great if you could memorize this so you are always reminded of the "new" you.

Ephesians 4:21-24 (NLT)
21Since you have heard about Jesus and have learned the truth that comes from him, 22throw off your old sinful nature and your former way of life, which is corrupted by lust and deception. 23Instead let the Spirit renew your thoughts and attitudes. 24Put on your new nature, created to be like God—truly righteous and holy.

5 MINUTES

Spend some time reviewing the following questions in relation to the verses you've just read. Write down your answers if it helps you concentrate.

- In your own words, how would you define "the truth that comes from Jesus"? How has Jesus' truth affected your life?

- Are you courageous enough to admit where your old and sinful way of life still has control of you? How do you feel about those things?

- How can we "throw off" our old way of living? What role do you think the Spirit might play in getting rid of the old—and what role do *you* play in that process?

- In what ways is the "new nature" described in today's passage an attractive image of what life with God could be like?

3 MINUTES

You and God

- Tell God what the last 30 days have been like for you. If you feel you know him more than ever, tell him that and thank him for his presence.

- If you are experiencing the joy of being made new, thank God's Spirit for doing that work in you, and thank Jesus for sending the Holy Spirit to dwell in us.

- Listen for a moment to hear if God is renewing your thoughts and attitudes even now.

THOUGHTS

This space is here for you to jot down some thoughts, write out a prayer, draw a picture, or do whatever you want to help you remember your 10-minute moment.